Career

Guide

An Expert's Guide to Building Your Block chain Career

(How to Become a Pathfinder for Lifetime Success & Fulfillment Career Planning)

Robert Hansen

Published By **Regina Loviusher**

Robert Hansen

Career Guide: An Expert's Guide to Building Your Block chain Career (How to Become a Pathfinder for Lifetime Success & Fulfillment Career Planning)

ISBN   978-1-998901-76-0

No part of this guidbook shall be reproduced in any form without permission in writing from the publisher except in the case of brief quotations embodied in critical articles or reviews.

Legal & Disclaimer

The information contained in this book is not designed to replace or take the place of any form of medicine or professional medical advice. The information in this book has been provided for educational & entertainment purposes only.

The information contained in this book has been compiled from sources deemed reliable, and it is accurate to the best of the Author's knowledge; however, the Author cannot guarantee its accuracy and validity and cannot be held liable for any errors or omissions. Changes are periodically made to this book. You must consult your doctor or get professional medical advice before using any of the suggested remedies, techniques, or information in this book.

Table of Contents

Chapter 1: Personal Branding

The Shortsightedness of Selling Yourself

How Personal Branding Is Messing with Your Mind

Everything on hand about hobby-searching tells you to promote your self, to clearly accept that you're a product and the employer is the consumer. Indeed, the resume is often known as a marketing record, honestly because the elevator pitch has been recast as your non-public emblem.

This advertising metaphor is uncomfortable to wear. People aren't products. No one desires to see themselves as a lower-wrapped widget. And proper right here's the worst thing: whilst you're selling a few aspect you don't believe in, you don't promote a whole lot of them!

If your assignment are seeking for isn't imparting you with thousands pass again, it's because of the truth you're stuck in promoting mode. No one desires to be sold to. Do you realize all people who gets obsessed on walking right into a vehicle dealership? Or being accosted thru a smarmy voice on a pop-up video?

You're no longer a product, and so long as you present like one, no man or woman's going to stroll onto your vehicle lot or click on on on your "Buy Now" button.

Being inauthentic might also moreover additionally turn some heads, however in the long run, it consequences in being worn-out, sour, and aloof, like a blow-hard salesman with a shtick that's not on foot. People can see right thru it, and it's miles messing along side your mind.

How to Undo the Voodoo of Branding

> Don't promote your self. Show your self.

A little little bit of a reframe is so as right proper here. Instead of seeing a interest are searching out as promoting yourself, think about it as an possibility to discover what you're absolutely approximately and keep that up for the area to appearance. Big difference. Selling yourself feels fake and drains you. Showing yourself feels proper and energizes you. Indeed, it transforms you.

Whenever you're feeling out of place or pissed off together together along with your technique are looking for, prevent searching out and as an possibility, look inward. Forget about the humans handy and get lower lower back to YOU. Answer a few of these questions and you'll find out your compass: Which artwork sports cause you to lose tune of time? What advice do people are seeking out from you? What may want to your preferred colleague say is your superpower? What should you do all day? In those answers, you'll find out the power of your tale.

> Test your tale to keep in mind your greatness.

The well information is the matters that make you superb are intertwined in some unspecified time in the future of your complete lifestyles. Take any of these achievements you simply got here up with and replicate on in advance levels of your life. I'll guess you may find a comparable tale, every in artwork and to your personal life. I comprehend this because of the reality I've been career education humans for years and there may be commonly a connection amongst beyond and present accomplishments. In order for you to tell a extremely good tale, you want to trust in your tale first. And information is your crystal ball.

> Trade your elevator pitch for an IM Intro.

Yes, your spiel need to be quick, but it shouldn't be corny or contrived. Speak as if you're writing a brief textual content to the organisation to tell them who you're. To live actual, act as if you're communicating with a pal of a pal. In fact, to check your IM Intro, try it on a friend. If you may't do it without feeling uncomfortable or self-conscious, that means it's not equipped but. You must be capable of introduce your self in your very non-public voice without the two of you busting out laughing. Keep it short, modest, and to be had. You're looking to start a conversation, not convince a person to drop the whole thing and rent you instant.

> You aren't a product.

Never attempt to be someone you're now not. You may be compelling definitely via the usage of telling human beings about the cool things you've finished. Pick your quality hits however permit yourself to be sincere and fallible. Get enthusiastic about your testimonies as they actually passed off. Let your art work speak for itself.

Chapter 2: Job Applications

Throwing Perfect Pitches right proper into a Black Hole

How Job Applications Are Messing with Your Mind

Imagine you're in the ninth inning of the World Series. You're throwing absolutely the excellent pitches you've ever thrown—satisfactory moves each time—but the umpire isn't calling them. Worse, the pitches seem to vanish as they flow into the plate. You can see that they're high-quality, however no man or woman else does.

Similarly, you're spending hours and hours discovering businesses, crafting cover letters, and reshaping your resume to align with the desires of the groups you're focused on. You fireplace the ones masterpieces downfield and listen not something in cross back, as although your properly-crafted resume is flying right now proper into a black hollow.

Shakespeare writes of Unrequited Love, in which the hero longs for an out-of-attain associate who doesn't reply. In your mission trying to find, you're experiencing Unrequited Job Interest.

You are desperately inquisitive about a device, but you're not getting some issue in move again. And no longer like Shakespeare's characters, you may in no way be capable of woo the object of your affection into loving you back. Romeo professes his love as soon as and complains about it for a whole play.

As a way seeker, you deliver your coronary coronary coronary heart out masses of instances, frequently with out a respond, and also you're anticipated to without a doubt deal with it. It's sincerely maddening, in all likelihood extra so than romance.

Like all and sundry, you want validation from others. This isn't always a prone point, but a popular stress. When you don't get keep of this validation, you start to question your credentials. If the dearth of validation keeps unchecked, you may draw the wrong cease which you're no longer definitely really worth of what you are attempting to find, that the universe is telling you to surrender, that there is a cause for all this silence. This is the uninvited effect that Unrequited Job Interest can also have on you.

How to Undo the Voodoo of the Application Process

> Come up on the facet of your very personal metric of achievement.

If you rely completely on getting callbacks due to the reality the identifying problem of your achievement, you're giving away control of your days. Instead, offer you with distinct metrics: fee your achievement by way of the form of programs you supply out in a day (which needn't be greater than 2 or 3 appropriate wonderful apps) or thru the use of locating at least 1 exceptional way opportunity whenever you sit all of the manner proper all the way down to do your research. Build your very personal yardstick.

> Routinely praise your hard work.

Job looking is a marathon of each day sprints. Remember to take a few victory laps. Each time you meet a metric you put for yourself, enjoy a praise. The rewards don't need to be big, simply frequent and healthy. Instead of gorging on an ice cream cone, hitting a bar, or binge-searching Netflix, drink tea with a pal, pass for a stroll, or allow yourself to test a wonderful ebook. A reward designates the a achievement stop of some issue. It's a outstanding way to transition out of activity-search mode and decrease again into your everyday lifestyles.

> Track your development.

You can't have any feel of fulfillment if you don't understand what you've completed. Whether a spreadsheet, a cell app, or Post-it Notes to your wall, make sure to song your packages from the start. Job searches can take 3-6 months or longer. It obtained't be lengthy earlier than you're no longer capable of do not forget all of the locations to which you carried out.

You can geek out on this part of your system seek as thousands or as little as you want to. There are severa commercial organisation merchandise and subscription offerings to be had. If you choose out to assemble your very personal tool, ensure to encompass the commercial enterprise agency, what excited you maximum about the activity, the date of the application, the dates of your observe-up correspondence, and a few region for notes. I'd suggest developing a separate tool for interview tracking.

> Optimize your electronic mail.

Make sure you operate a expert-sounding e-mail deal with. Consider growing a emblem-new alias devoted to your mission searching for. That manner, you can set up filters to set up your correspondence and ensure not anything vital is going into your junk mail folder.

> Follow the suggestions!

You acquired't get thru in case you don't play with the resource of the policies. Follow the software commands exactly as they're written, however the fact that they sound ridiculous. Rejection is a lot extra tragic in case you're a brilliant in form but you gave away your shot due to the fact your software program end up in no manner reviewed.

Chapter 3: Job Boards

A Beacon of Nope

How Job Boards Are Messing with Your Mind

If the utility approach is a black hole, then interest boards are like a neon yellow flashing arrow pointing to the middle of that black hole. They are siren requires Unrequited Job Interest. The chance you'll get a callback is narrow. Worse, you may get a callback for a interest you don't even need, one which undervalues you and motives you to question your very own properly nicely worth.

Job boards are the very first-class and most famous approach of looking for artwork, because of this they're additionally the maximum competitive place to look for artwork and, consequently, the least probable location that you're going to discover art work. By a long way.

Somewhere among 2%-three% of jobs are filled via technique boards.

It's the final hotel for employers, and but most people spend hours at a time trolling thru pastime listings, casting a internet some distance and large along hundreds of various novice fishermen with their eye at the same shimmering lure.

If job forums are your primary or simplest channel of utilizing for jobs, then you definately're no longer getting a diverse pattern of feedback. As a stop end result, you're more likely to simply accept as true with what you pay interest, from whoever really calls you once more, despite the fact that they've have been given the incorrect idea approximately you and that they're simply seeking to suit you in a discipline.

The fruitlessness of hobby forums erodes at your self perception and lures you away from your center values in searching out paintings. You may also moreover begin to assume you've been searching within the incorrect region. You'll question how a terrific deal you recognize, what you need to offer, and whether or not or no longer or no longer you're properly well worth an enterprise business enterprise's time.

It occurs to the first rate people.

How to Undo the Voodoo of Job Boards

> Diversify your seek.

You need to certainly positioned your resume up on project forums and installation a few ticklers to warn you to accurate system listings coming down the pike, however don't troll the forums for hours on give up.

Job boards ought to be a small aspect of your multi-faceted attack. Set a timer and spend no more than 30-45 mins/day with a small series of 3-five project forums.

Use superb strategies of discovering method opportunities, along with (tele)meetings, meetups (virtual or in any other case), volunteering, business enterprise associations and listservs, espresso chats, LinkedIn (see monetary ruin nine), other social media, network boards, Q&A forums, commercial enterprise corporation internet websites, organization media, mainstream press, alumni networks, new trainings, professor/teacher guidelines, 0.33-birthday celebration recruiters (see financial disaster eight), and location professionals to call a few.

Most importantly, make sure to form your day with offline sports activities to balance out the thumb-in depth trolling and scrolling.

> Spy earlier than you purchase.

When you word an possibility on a process board, hold off on making use of, in particular in case you're wonderful interested in it.

Do a few studies. Google the employer. Scour their internet net page. Find today's press on them outside in their internet net page. Check out what employees are saying on Glassdoor. Discover what the business business enterprise is satisfied with and what they're struggling with.

Then, see if you could find out who's doing the hiring and stalk them on the Internet and social media. Go a chunk deeper and notice if the satisfaction endures.

> Apply to the corporation without delay.

Even if hobby forums flip up an opportunity, don't look at thru them, because you'll be setting your self along hundreds of numerous applicants.

Instead, go to the commercial enterprise employer's net site and study if you can find out the task opportunity there. Better however, network your manner to an worker or alumnus of the employer via LinkedIn or through your very private circle of pals. Use your diligent research to make a excellent advent and butter up your influential new contact.

Chapter 4: Job Listings

In the Shadow of Unicorns and Purple Squirrels

How Job Listings Are Messing with Your Mind

Job listings are designed to make you experience inadequate. They describe the appropriate candidate, a person who possibly doesn't exist. Indeed, recruiters—who spend their days looking for the ones taking walks-speaking demigods—created a call for them: the purple squirrel. Like unicorns, crimson squirrels are a adorable photo that doesn't exist.

There is a reason hiring managers model a procedure listing after the elusive crimson squirrel, beyond simply hoping to find out one. An exceptional gadget listing serves hiring managers properly within the income negotiation section when you remember that they may element to qualifications that you're lacking and provide less coins. They additionally reduce the chances of complaints.

So, approach descriptions work for the enterprise. What does it do for you?

Reviewing task descriptions is like binge-looking a YouTube channel of top-engaging in Bodybuilders and Brainiacs. The first-rate turns into the not unusual. When you look down at your very personal everyday self, in area of feeling pumped up, you turn out to be rundown. In evaluating your self to the purple squirrels, you slip from engaging in to aspirational.

As a forestall end result, you can chorus from utilising to some of those jobs and even as you do look at through on using, you're probably to be lukewarm on yourself-photo.

How to Undo the Voodoo of Job Listings

> Remember that no individual is a squirrel.

It's so clean to think in reality all people else is extra licensed than you, but specific candidates are probably scratching their heads at the task requirements as nicely. Recognize that pink squirrels are pretty unusual or even if there may be one to be had, the threat they'll be discovered, to be had, and espresso-price is statistically quite low. So, even if you're not checking all the boxes on the activity listing but you're enthusiastic about the region, observe besides!

> Note the order of things.

With pastime listings, the most vital and non-negotiable stuff is at the pinnacle. Pay interest to the pinnacle 3-four objects below Job Duties and Requirements. If you don't have the ones capabilities or attributes, rethink using. However, if you've have been given all of the topics at the top, however are missing a few in the course of the lowest, don't get too discouraged. Apply besides, and study with vigor.

> Ingest the important thing terms.

Job listings are a keyword goldmine. The corporation is supplying you with the answers to the take a look at. Take the time to soak them up.

The terms utilized in activity listings have to turn out to be part of your lexicon. You can brief create a draw close list of the jargon to your enterprise thru reviewing 3-4 interest listings and writing down all of the key phrases; there are generally about 10-20 consistent with listing. You'll word that there is a lot of overlap throughout all the listings. This is a superb issue.

Here's a trick a number of resume writers use: in case you actually need to geek out on keywords, drop the content material cloth fabric of 5-10 goal process listings into a "phrase cloud" device to get a visible diagram showcasing which key phrases are maximum often used and, consequently, maximum important as a way to ingest into your presentation, on paper and in character.

> Address the hidden requirement.

Don't certainly take a look at what's written; have a test the way it's written. This will give you a window into the way of lifestyles of the organization. Are they snarky? Corporate? Casual? Creative? Hyperbolic? Warm?

Mirror this temper to your correspondence with the agency. In hiring, attitude trumps nearly the entirety else. Attitude denotes culture healthy and all organizations prioritize retaining their cherished manner of existence intact. As a former recruiter, I'm right right here to mention you can beat out a crimson squirrel in case you go with the flow in with the right thoughts-set.

Chapter 5: Resumes

Tweaking the Mona Lisa

How Resume Editing Is Messing with Your Mind

Can you trust looking to persuade an artist to redo her art work for really every person that walked into the gallery? What if we advised a journalist to rewrite his weblog positioned up constant with who visits his net website online? Ludicrous! Yet, this is precisely what's expected people as method seekers.

Resumes are masterpieces. They're self-pictures of your quality component. An awesome paintings of artwork. And they take pretty a bargain as prolonged to create as any of da Vinci's achievements.

But, no longer just like the exquisite Mona Lisa, resumes are by no means finished. You are continuously tweaking your resume, or at the least you're alleged to be, on every occasion you comply with for a present day-day function.

It's any other brick in the road of the most effective-sided uphill climb that is going with any technique are looking for: you're counseled to hold converting yourself. This isn't healthful. No one desires to date or paintings with a chameleon.

Every time you tweak your resume, you're chipping away a chunk of your self and filling it with a specific piece. In time, you'll stray up to now from the authentic masterpiece that you'll be looking an ambiguous rockpile. Tweak your resume sufficient instances and in sufficient suggestions, and also you'll destroy your spirit.

Following are some quick strategies to edit your resume so you can avoid recreating the Mona Lisa on every occasion you spot a job you want.

How to Undo the Voodoo of Resume Editing

> Change the primary 3 phrases.

The best content material material you need to constantly trade to your resume is the primary few phrases, which must be a characteristic identify that lines up with the goal venture to be had.

If your pick out is Program Manager and the undertaking you're making use of for is Senior Project Manager, keep in thoughts changing the previous to the latter. A phrase of warning: appearance out for splendid-particular undertaking titles. For instance, if a enterprise is advertising and advertising for a Head of Anti-Chaos Engineering, without a doubt go along with Operations Manager. You want to seem like a extraordinary match, now not like a person who is making an attempt desperately to appear to be a fantastic healthy.

> Don't rewrite. Reshuffle.

Instead of rewriting everything, focus on shifting complete sections spherical, putting the most applicable stuff better on the internet net page.

Reorder the bullet elements in every method, restack the key phrases in your abilities list, trade the gathering of your technical skills, and reprioritize the bullets in your summary segment, when you have one. This way, you'll be catering your content cloth to the venture description with out losing your story (and yourself!) inside the machine.

> Slash your interest titles.

Keyword bots are clever. They understand in which to find technique titles on a resume. To thwart the bots, revel in loose to provide yourself 2 or perhaps 3 key-phrase-rich activity titles, separated thru a in advance lessen. For instance, allow's say you're a Marketing Coordinator but you want a manner that focuses on marketplace research. You might probably use "Marketing Coordinator / Market Research Analyst" as your new discover. If asked about it inside the interview, say that you protected your actual activity call similarly on your beneficial pastime title that higher explains what you do. This reduce method works tremendous for LinkedIn profiles as properly.

> Change your style.

This one is non-obligatory, however often overlooked.

Color subjects, particularly if you're the usage of for your dream company. You can find the RGB and HEX shade palettes of public companies thru doing a short internet search. Only trade the color of your name, headings, and/or interest titles. Don't use greater than 2 colorations.

> Hire a pro from the get-pass.

The satisfactory expert resume writers will create a resume that's with out problem "update-succesful," that means, you'll be capable of tailor your resume for a hobby list in 2 minutes or heaps tons much less.

Chapter 6: Cover Letters

So Many Introductions, So Little Time

How Cover Letters Are Messing with Your Mind

You're at a celebration or on an app and each unmarried man or woman wants to meet you and they all want you to be the most exciting person they've ever met. Oh, and that they're fine supplying you with some seconds to make your introduction. Ready… pass!

Tweaking the resume is tedious sufficient. Now you need to recreate but a few distinct document that sincerely reiterates your capabilities all another time. Is this definitely crucial?

Yes, cowl letters are although a difficulty.

Not all hiring mother and father need to appearance them but a few do, this means that that you need to create one for every way opportunity. The unfortunate issue proper here is that, no longer like your resume, this masterpiece can also never get have a study. Still, you want to obsess over it like some other artwork of art work, lest your hiring manager could likely swipe left on you.

You are, of route, thrilling however it gets tiring identifying a manner to be exciting to all people, specially thru writing. And it's even greater disillusioning even as you preserve in mind that your goal market— the organization—is "meeting" a set extra people in advance than and after you, every with the identical purpose of being the maximum thrilling.

It's daunting. The problem is if you're bored writing however another cover letter, humans are going to be bored reading it.

How to Undo the Voodoo of Cover Letters

> Create a quick, non-tacky lead-in.

Consider kicking off the letter with a right away, short, conversational assertion that illustrates your charge proposition actually. For example, "I make sure responsibilities end on time" or "Data is my life" or "Companies that assume earlier pop out earlier." Distilling your essence like this can assist you awareness and will wake your reader from their stupor.

> Keep it brief.

Good statistics! Cover letters are becoming shorter, possibly due to the fact hiring managers' attention spans and the allotted time to look for candidates have reduced in size as nicely.

In your first paragraph, point out your years of revel in in the enterprise and inside the position, making sure it strains up with what they're looking for. Then, have 3-5 bullet points that cope with the salient duties and necessities at the aim activity description. You want to show you're certified issue-for-factor. Conclude with a thank-you and the same old "I appearance beforehand to assembly you" remark.

Even with the quick cover letter format, you have to customise it for every process, which includes an intro paragraph that talks about why you're inquisitive about the business enterprise and the position.

> Explain away some component sticky.

Create a longer letter if you need to give an explanation for a few component for your paintings statistics.

For instance, if you have 2 or three careers taking walks in parallel, show how they suit together. If you have have been given a system out of doors of your dominant career, percentage the way it's applicable. If you're creating a profession transition, provide an purpose for why you're well equipped to do so. If you have got an uncommon paintings statistics, make the case why it makes you an top notch better candidate.

You can't do these things with a resume, in its restricted format. That's why the cover letter is a golden opportunity to maintain those items in to the talk. Don't look ahead to the enterprise to say those devices. Instead, get the communication began out now, for your personal flattering words, after which stop it up inside the interview.

> Include a postscript.

P.S. Stands for "postscript" and postscripts continually get examine. People are certainly too curious.

Good content material fabric material for a postscript includes a quick testimonial from a supervisor, a quote you like, your very very own succinct art work philosophy, purpose in the lower back of a nickname you've got, a completely particular challenge you finished, a weird accolade or award, a a laugh truth approximately your self, or a "congrats" on modern-day press approximately the reason enterprise.

Chapter 7: Networking

You Schmooze, You Lose

How Networking Is Messing with Your Mind

The number one way to get a task is to apprehend someone. This undisputed little statistic is the birthplace of Networking — the mechanism we use to emerge as someone who knows someone. The charge of networking is so pervasive and universally acquainted that whole industries have sprouted up spherical it. Tons of organizations have networking on the heart of their enterprise company model, alongside facet social media internet websites, executive matching corporations, and convention facilities.

There is one problem: nearly nobody likes networking, specifically in man or woman. And only a few human beings like networkers. Everyone is aware about after they're being networked. It's stressful.

It doesn't don't forget how properly the pitch is or how exciting the branding assertion is (e.G., "I make ordinary humans inclusive of you into millionaires in a single day!"), you apprehend whilst it's taking location to you and it never feels accurate. You can be listening in self-hobby or out of hobby or maybe out of envy, however now not due to the fact you surely enjoy an affinity with this individual.

A actual connection isn't always possible via a shtick. Deep down, you recognize this to be real, it clearly is why you hate networking.

Networking places you once more within the "dealer" mind-set, that is uncomfortable for maximum mother and father. Networking moreover tends to make us experience needy and insecure (e.G., "I'm so desperate for paintings, I'm begging strangers for a activity"). And for the ones introverts to be had, networking is frequently considered an real living hell. Don't agree with me? Just ask the person hovering over the punchbowl.

The bottom line is you actually need to be networking, but how do you get to a place in which you really want to participate in this required hobby-are searching for ritual?

How to Undo the Voodoo of Networking

> Ditch the pitch.

Canned responses suck. People might as a substitute pay attention you fumble spherical in an proper way, than supply polished prefab answers to their questions.

I'm fine you'd agree that the first rate bridal ceremony vows and graduation speeches are unscripted and incorporate stuttering, crying, and mistakes. That's due to the fact awkwardness denotes vulnerability and vulnerability is what makes us enjoy inside the direction of one another.

> Talk about some issue else.

Your counterpart is more likely to keep in mind your heat tub tale than your branding assertion. Remember, you're simply searching for to make a actual connection; it doesn't should be about your brand or your product.

Instead, strive speaking approximately your breakfast, your excursion, your youngsters, your entrepreneurial struggles... Speak from the coronary

coronary heart. My fail-regular opener for networking is to ask someone how their morning went. It offers me a window into the character's existence within the right right here and now. They don't see it coming, so they supply a real answer. And we're off in the proper route.

> Give to get.

A golden rule of powerful networking is "Give to Get."

It feels exact to be of company and people reciprocate generosity instinctively. So, think about how you can assist this individual. Tell them approximately a piece of writing you without a doubt check, a podcast they have to check out, a chum who had a comparable trouble, a e-book you heard approximately.

Become a beneficial useful resource and watch the enterprise corporation gambling cards and textual content messages come flying. They won't offer you a challenge in that 2nd, but on the same time as you attain out to them, they'll reply. That's what networking is all approximately. The "Give to Get" technique works substantially well for LinkedIn, too. More on this later.

> Network with humans you understand.

It doesn't constantly have to be with strangers. A sad truth is that we no longer often speak approximately our careers with friends and own family, other than venting and complaining. If you're like maximum people, your friends slightly recognize what you do, or how well you do it. It's time to make a mobile phone date and change that.

Remember, no elevator pitches. Explain a undertaking you loved jogging on, share your starting place story. And invite them to percentage theirs. Make new connections with antique contacts.

Chapter 8: Interviewing

Dancing Naked for Complete Strangers

How Interviewing Is Messing with Your Mind

My graduate professor wrote a e book on interviewing titled Dancing Naked due to the truth that's what it looks as if at the same time as you're attempting to impress folks which might be firing questions at you need they're taking pictures bullets at your toes.

Dancing naked in personal is brilliant, certainly, restoration! But dancing naked within the front of strangers, properly…

it's literally the stuff nightmares are made from.

Most human beings see interviewing as a strength exercise in which the hiring manager and her effective inquisition team have all of the strength and maintain all of the playing playing cards. They stand among you and your very very own prosperity, with that "What are you gonna do for me?" appearance on their faces and a six-shooter complete of hole-tipped "gotcha" questions.

Very few parents absolutely appearance in advance to interviewing, but the ones who do are extraordinarily a achievement. You can be that character.

How to Undo the Voodoo of Interviewing

> Remember your power.

We regularly neglect about that the character on the other component of the desk is hoping to find you as lots as you're hoping to discover them.

As a former recruiter, I can let you know hiring managers want the undertaking are trying to find to surrender. ASAP. They're banking on you—their subsequent interviewee—to make that take area. That's your strength.

And proper right right here's a few more power: regardless of how first-rate you accept as true with you studied this machine is, there are greater jobs accessible which is probably equal to it or higher. The math is to your decide upon. They want you actually as hundreds, if not extra, than you want them.

> Interview them back.

The interview is a two-way avenue.

Instead of dancing naked, ask some questions your self. Go into the interview with an agenda: three-four elements you'll make irrespective of their questions. This time desk will floor you. It's your property base. You'll never clean out since you'll commonly have something to transport once more to.

Rather than sitting there thinking "I choice they select me," flip it round. Think "Is this organization top enough for me? How can they assist me?"

And, on the forestall of the interview, use the subsequent query to discover how you did, earlier than you go away the interview. Ask "What character tendencies make a person successful in this function?" They will maintain to inform you precisely what they need to appearance in a candidate and you could take a look at your art work to fill in any clean spots you may not have covered but. It works like a allure and you go away feeling like one million greenbacks.

> Lead with enthusiasm, and boatloads of it.

The interview isn't always the time in your poker face. Let your ardour flag fly. Make positive you're genuinely stoked approximately the opportunity on at least four ranges: the corporation, the company, the life-style, and the placement. And be prepared to share this delight, whether or now not they ask you approximately those objects or now not.

If you're feeling along side you're faking your way into pride, then admit that this challenge isn't always for you, and now not surely nicely worth your valuable time. Or theirs.

> Accept that you could in no manner know why.

There are plenty of reasons why agencies say NO, most of which do not have a few aspect to do with you. They also can have an internal hire, they will have misplaced the fee range, they'll have pivoted in a present day route, they may have changed manage.

Definitely ask for comments, however apprehend it isn't always in the enterprise's first rate interest to provide it to you. They chance litigation. So, don't push it. Accept it. Be gracious. And circulate on.

Chapter 9: Recruiters

Kneeling Before the Gatekeepers

How Recruiters Are Messing with Your Mind

You can see the golden city inside the distance — a jeweled and sparkling land wherein promise and opportunity abound. Alas, the metropolis is gated and the elusive gatekeeper flitters beyond the entrance, twirling the keys spherical his finger, seemingly bored with you and the road of website site visitors inside the returned of you, clutching at their packs.

Talk approximately energy! Recruiters, much like citadel guards, have all of the keys. They have all the jobs, however for some reason, they don't appear to have all that a whole lot time for challenge seekers.

You emerge as feeling like an outsider, regardless of how darned licensed you recognize yourself to be. Recruiter feedback can be cryptic and blunt, which can go away you thinking your credentials. Everyone seems to recognize more than you do. Everyone's speaking to each different about you however, come what might also, you're no longer inside the communique.

How to Undo the Voodoo of Recruiters

> Don't hate the player, hate the sport.

Here's what's within the lower back of the recruiter hustle: the tons much much less time a recruiter takes to fill a characteristic, the extra money they make.

Most recruiters are contingency recruiters, aka 1/three-birthday party recruiters; they paintings for the corporation, no longer for you. Nothing private. It's the organization who is handing them a 20% price take a look at closer to your profits.

You, of course, have the selection of hiring a Retained Search Firm in which you pay the recruiter your self, but maximum method seekers pick no longer to make investments tens of lots of dollars in a hobby are searching for, especially whilst they're no longer running. So, be satisfied you're getting a free company, however truncated or rushed it may be.

> Talk to many, not one.

Just as recruiters artwork with many interest seekers without delay, you have to paintings with numerous recruiters. Set up a network of search/placement professionals to growth your odds and equalize the electricity dynamic. And don't limit your self to jogging with neighborhood looking for corporations. A recruiter may additionally moreover recruit for the New York marketplace but live in Palm Springs for the life-style.

> Use a broking.

If you're in search of to get inside the the front of a ton of recruiters in a unmarried day, don't forget operating with a resume-writing organisation; numerous resume writers offer Resume Distribution Services that supply your resume to loads, even plenty, of recruiters with the click of a button. Recruiters price sturdy resumes — they may be attempting to find for out professional resume writers due to the reality they apprehend they'll be able to galvanize their portfolio of agencies.

> Know what you want.

Recruiters will respect you immensely if you come to them clean on what you want to offer and what you could do for his or her companies. And once they appreciate you, they're much more likely to hook you up, so have your tale proper away.

> Digest the hard comments.

In the lonely expanse of nonresponsiveness at some point of your undertaking are in search of, feedback is food. And recruiter remarks is filet mignon. Be humble and gracious, in spite of the most harsh of critics. Rejection is hard, however if a recruiter takes the time to inform you why you didn't make the cut, it manner they anticipate you're properly actually well worth it ultimately.

Chapter 10: Linkedin

Your Life Story on a Billboard in Times Square

How LinkedIn Is Messing with Your Mind

Writing your lifestyles's tale is tough enough, however whilst you understand for a reality that loads of human beings are going to be comparing your tale in a public forum, it receives even greater ominous. Everybody's searching!

To add greater weight to the mission, you are compelled to install writing a single profile for yourself, no matter how many hobbies, careers, aspirations, and activity searches you have got have been given occurring.

Human beings are complicated. The most exciting and certified human beings have twists and turns of their paintings histories, nuances to their roles, fortuitous errors, and typically a couple of man or woman they gift to the arena. LinkedIn calls for that each one of these complexities collapse into one nicely prepared charge proposition.

This is a frightening assignment. Trying to distill your self proper right into a monolithic machine candidate can depart you feeling one-dimensional, incomplete, exposed, misrepresented, or maybe dishonest — no longer the exquisite headspace to be in on your interest are seeking for!

Further, you may not similar to the idea of "bragging" approximately yourself and your accomplishments. The belief of tooting your personal horn goes in the direction of your grain, and doing it in a public discussion board makes gambling that tune all the greater uncomfortable.

How to Undo the Voodoo of LinkedIn

> Pick your voice.

Before you even begin writing, do that workout: on a scale of 1 to 10 with 1 being begin-up informal and 10 being organization expert, write down the variety that designates the way you need to be perceived. Consider your company, your function, and your region while making this feature.

Once you decide to a unmarried voice, you'll revel in greater targeted in terms of the manner you need to write down. From proper right here, you can circulate at once to what you're going to install writing.

> Use the precis on your advantage.

The Summary phase is an open-ended invitation to mention a few issue you need. Use this on your advantage. Yes, you have to stuff heaps of keywords into your precis, however moreover take the opportunity to present an reason for the trickier topics on your paintings records.

The LinkedIn summary is an extraordinary opportunity inside the project-are seeking out method to get a piece non-public. Unless you're an employer luminary who "wishes no introduction", take a second to allow people understand who you clearly are.

> Use your resume as a manual.

Do your resume first. If you're in a rush, really reduce-and-paste sections of your resume into your profile. That can tide you over for some time. When you have extra time, try and summarize subjects a chunk and in shape your Experience and

Education sections with your preferred "voice." As a famous rule, your LinkedIn profile should be shorter, extra private, and extra modest than your resume.

Having your resume and LinkedIn profile aligned will leave you feeling complete, for you to decorate your self-self assurance and self-efficacy.

> Have your allies chime in.

Once you've knowledgeable your story, invite your colleagues to validate it. With LinkedIn, you could do this thru guidelines and endorsements. Remember the "Give to Get" rule of networking? Use it with LinkedIn: deliver a person else a recommendation and that they'll most likely reciprocate.

> Show your image.

A image is nicely nicely worth 1000 words. Make positive you have got a wonderful, near-up profile % that is not too polished however now not too informal. And change your historical past image from the default format to a few aspect that famous your hobbies, area, and/or aspirations.

Prepare yourself for the long time

Whether you joined the organisation as a sparkling graduate or as a expert rent, after a few years you'll discover your early benefit behind you. To make that subsequent breakthrough you need to apprehend more approximately how businesses paintings after which use that data to enhance your feature. This bankruptcy will assist you.

A profession is normally measured in a long time no longer in weeks or months. Whatever level you are at to your profession it's far essential to be organized for the long term. Actions you're taking in recent times might not supply fruit straight away, it is able to take months or years. Preparing for the long term will boom the possibilities of career development while the opportunities arise.

Advancement

Corporates are competitive locations. At any factor in time, your colleagues is probably chasing all of the opportunities whilst you're left in the back of doing the paintings. Try to grow to be aware of the distinction amongst there being no relevant possibilities for you within the suggest time and achieving a profession plateau in which new possibilities will rarely stand up.

At any factor to your career, you can enjoy that not something new or exciting has took place for some time and you've reached a plateau. This often takes location with folks that want to turn out to be professionals due to the reality they benefit a aspect in which there can be no clean next float upwards while remaining a professional. If you opt to specialize then that may be okay for you.

Otherwise, in case you see yourself at the manipulate career path then you definately virtually don't want to plateau. Always be geared up for opportunities and intention for advertising and marketing.

People

Get to apprehend your supervisor higher. Try to recognize his motivation, what is he seeking out, what appears to satisfaction him. You don't need to turn out to be exquisite of pals with him but it assist you to masses to apprehend his point of view. One thing of this is to get to recognise greater approximately his boss and what he expects of him.

Find allies inside the business agency business enterprise. Your allies may be your pals who paintings in one in every of a kind factors of the organisation or they'll sincerely be human beings which you have helped and that they need to move once more the pick. With allies, you are looking for human beings that assist you to at the same time as needed. Otherwise, your scope of effect is probably no bigger than the organization you are in and in case you want to leave that crew then you'll be absolutely unsupported out of doors.

Ideally, your allies will act as unofficial individual witnesses while everyone mentions you or asks what you're like.

It is constantly a remarkable technique to additionally have precise relationships with some people outdoor your manipulate hierarchy. A specially critical company of human beings to be aware of are the non-public assistants of the senior managers. These humans control get right of entry to to the manager and if they prefer then you definately definately without a doubt they will be more likely to tell you in which he's or to squeeze you into his time table for a 5-minute chat at the identical time as you want it. Furthermore, many managers ask the opinion in their assistants when they want to understand extra about a person. So having a extraordinary dating enables.

Learn to tolerate and be affected character with humans which you don't like. One way or every other you all need to art work collectively. Don't hold a grudge. The individual you dislike might also moreover come to be your boss, in any other case you grow to be his boss. Keep it cordial and professional.

Be aware that even inside the same institution as you, the overall performance and productiveness of every person will range wildly. Getting a big organization of humans to artwork together can be very inefficient in contrast to at least one expert operating on their very very own. Even the productivity of one plus one not frequently equals . However, that is the model selected with the resource of huge corporates. The superb you could do is to phrase who does what inside the group and who will allow you to.

Similarly, the profile of the managers you will meet in a company will range a high-quality deal too. Agencies will normally have a few extraordinary managers, masses of common managers and some poor managers. Often the horrible managers are folks that lack the competencies to manipulate or have been exceeded over for advertising and marketing so regularly that they will be now demotivated beyond repair. Then there are managers you will meet who will go away you wondering if they are virtually managers or if they will be politicians. They may lack organization and venture manipulate abilties but their capability to control upward to senior manage ensures they will be normally seen in an extremely good mild.

A properly supervisor will do his first-rate to create an surroundings in which his organization can thrive. This may also additionally propose protective them from company politics, putting strain on exceptional companies to deliver what you want or preventing for the assets your group needs.

Your research into the humans and lifestyle of the commercial enterprise employer need to never prevent. People are a very essential part of working in a massive corporation.

Aim for selling

All people who be a part of a primary organization are looking for career increase or profession development. In my some years of employment, I need to anticipate one hand the form of human beings I even have met who had no ambition the least bit for their characteristic to evolve. One of the motives for this is that there are various methods to go through in thoughts career development and boom. This may additionally embody the following.

• Improved method pick out

- Increase in compensation

- Going up in the business organization chart

- Higher corporation score/elegance

- Having a bigger finances

- Increased autonomy

- Managing extra humans

- Moving to a wealthy location

- Changing united states or city

People often communicate approximately "hiking the corporation ladder". This refers to 1 type of career development in which there can be an imaginary direction from your entry point within the business enterprise as a good buy as being the pinnacle of the enterprise organization. In practical phrases, if a person works for a guide feature then in desire to trekking the ladder to end up the top of the organization it is more likely to be interpreted as turning into the top in their precise help function, e.G. Beginning as an accounting clerk and aiming to grow to be the Chief Financial Officer.

In some businesses, this path has described steps. They may also have a company grading scheme in which each worker is assigned to a particular level inside the corporation which corresponds to a specific rung on the ladder for that business business enterprise. In many distinct businesses, the task name illustrates in which someone is within the enterprise and in which they'll circulate to next; e.G. If a person is junior vice chairman then they realize that the following advertising will take them to vp, director and then handling director. In a few different agencies, the technique titles provide little indication of wherein they will be within the hierarchy. In which case to appearance the ladder it's far essential to observe the contemporary-day employer chart to look which roles there are a number of the man or woman's modern function and the pinnacle of the company chart.

Alternatively, there are unique employees who additionally need profession boom but they don't see themselves as ever on foot the commercial company company or being the top of their service characteristic. For example, inside the Information Technology department, there can be folks who want to emerge as experts in their own technical subject and that they need to be identified for it however they don't want to become the top of the department. They don't see themselves at the traditional enterprise ladder but they will be even though looking for possibilities and promotions.

How an extended way you could pass at the professional or alternative direction frequently relies upon whether or no longer or now not your characteristic is a part of the middle industrial corporation of your corporation. For example, in a prescription drugs company organization there might be very immoderate profile roles for the top research scientists. However, an open deliver technology expert will now not have many alternative profession direction options in a retail economic institution.

In conclusion, we have diagnosed unique profession paths: the conventional path of mountain climbing the company ladder and the opportunity path of receiving reputation for professional capabilities that are not on the traditional company ladder.

The human beings on every the conventional and the possibility profession paths would be pleased to gather an progressed machine call. In the traditional case, the superior procedure choose out may also mirror hiking similarly up the company ladder and within the possibility case, the machine identify would growth their popularity as a expert.

Compensation will growth can also or won't be synchronized with a sophisticated manner name or improvement up the profession ladder. Sometimes reimbursement will growth stand up unexpectedly because of the truth the business employer has determined out that the compensation being paid interior their organization for precise roles is so much a bargain much less than that being paid within the marketplace that they experience that a hard and fast in their employees are prone to defecting to their opposition. There are other agencies with a strict grading machine in which it might not be viable to increase someone's grade with out increasing their compensation; which may also additionally require a fee range growth approval. They can also have strict regulations bringing up what the maximum and minimum growth need to be.

Being seen to move up within the business enterprise chart is at once analogous to the traditional perception of trekking the business employer ladder. Those looking for opportunity career paths might be less interested by this type of progression till the improvement is within a consultant a part of the commercial enterprise employer chart.

Managing extra human beings does now not infer a direct boom in agency grade or even going up in the agency organisation chart. Many professionals say that the quantity of humans you control isn't related to your importance in the organisation or without delay associated with your repayment and that those are old notions. In my revel in, being given the hazard to control more human beings is a long time lever towards hiking the commercial enterprise agency ladder. That is to mention that irrespective of the truth that your end up aware of or your compensation isn't probably to exchange proper now, within the long time it is going to be identified which you are performing a greater crucial function for the agency than you have been in advance than and consequently your call, reimbursement, and grade will growth through the years.

Moving to a dynamic new employer region need to come to be a catalyst for profession increase. If you're a salesclerk and you circulate to an area of the business enterprise this is positioned to extremely boom in sales then your compensation have to dramatically growth via turning into a member of that area and being a achievement. This can be defined as a sideways skip as it does not include straight away mountain climbing the corporation ladder however it may well cause faster increase in some time. If your long term interest is greater approximately mountaineering the ladder than proper now growing your repayment then this form of circulate has its risks.

For example, if humans count on you have got were given grow to be successful not through your private endeavors however genuinely due to the fact you have been carried along with the aid of the area which you are in then you definately definately virtually won't be recognized for merchandising that brief. Alternatively, if you observe loads from the experience then senior control may also recognize that you may supply similar success to special regions if you have been given the possibility.

Sometimes, changing managers can create the enhance that your profession needs. Learn approximately one-of-a-kind managers in the agency. You may additionally moreover moreover have touch with a particularly encouraging and knowledgeable manager; while you communicate more you may discover that he has a function open. Managers are best human and loads of them can get the notable out of exquisite humans and now not others. Can you spot a better wholesome for you than together together with your contemporary supervisor?

Changing the u . S . A . Or the metropolis in which you art work for the agency need to turn out to be a leap up the company ladder, a remarkable long term sideways float or a completely interesting enjoy that doesn't at once help your potentialities. It very lots is predicated upon on the situations of the project. Global organizations hire neighborhood personnel of their operations round the world however they often need to have some of folks that convey the headquarters enterprise culture to the community operation too. This technique that there are often possibilities for middle managers to transport to every different region in which they may become the pinnacle in their department, this is an fantastic career opportunity as it lets in the individual to demonstrate that they could run a branch and that they have got to expect to be promoted once they go back.

In my enjoy, the factors maximum affecting getting a merchandising (of the conventional or possibility type) are:

• Completing all your responsibilities properly

• Getting observed

• Showing capability to do extra

There would possibly never be any speak approximately merchandising if you couldn't entire all the obligations which have been assigned to you. This is the minimum that every body have to ask. If your list of responsibilities is quite numerous then I might possibly rewrite this primary element as trying to complete all your immoderate profile duties nicely. That is to say, if humans extensively apprehend that you are accountable for positive things then those are the sports that should be finished nicely and on time to preserve and grow your accurate name.

Consider any non-public regulatory compliance duties to be very excessive profile. You may be requested to carry out a little thing mind-numbing that could be a distraction out of your important responsibilities, but failing to complete the ones responsibilities might be career restricting.

Unfortunately, it's far possible to art work tough and supply all your tasks yr after yr without getting promoted. To break out this situation you want to get located. This can also additionally seem selfish however your supervisor and any inner customers need to understand that it end up you and your groups that finished the ones successes. This is wherein you moreover might also need a healthful courting together together with your supervisor, he desires to experience that he can congratulate you in public on your achievements and that thru doing that it'll mirror well on him too. If he sees you as a threat then he might not need human beings to realize what you've got got finished.

If your manager does experience threatened by the usage of you, and perhaps you enjoy that you are higher than him, then you definitely want to think very carefully what your next steps will be to get that marketing and advertising and marketing that you are after. There is an antique announcing which you need to typically appearance after your supervisor and he will look when you. Approaching human beings above your manager can be very volatile in your profession, your manager may additionally want to have many more opportunities than you to offer an purpose at the back of himself to his supervisor and in evaluation, you may fine get one hazard. Console your self with the concept that most humans leapfrog their managers at the career ladder via a few smart sideways actions, now not through taking their role or by using the usage of becoming their boss.

If you're finishing all of your responsibilities and all and sundry who topics is privy to about it, however you're despite the fact that now not getting promoted; then query whether or not humans take transport of as genuine with you've got got the capacity to do more than you're. If you get the whole thing completed nicely and however you frequently make a drama approximately how difficult it's been, the way you don't virtually have the critical belongings or what number of extra hours you have got needed to installed every day then it's miles now not going that people will count on you have got extra functionality. I am not suggesting which you cover the more hours you've got were given were given worked or which you maintain quiet about the resourcing troubles, but you can need to re-frame the manner you communicate the ones factors.

When you're provided a promoting, by means of the usage of definition, it's far going to be to perform a little issue one-of-a-type from what you're already doing. For example, you might be asked to control the group you are already in or take over an area that everybody is aware of is in hassle. Regardless of the state of affairs, you may have no actual desire however to virtually get hold of the selling and then make the most of it. If you say no, then you definately can not be requested yet again.

Essential information about profession appraisals

The HR department in every most critical business organisation will run a profession appraisal software each 3 hundred and sixty five days (or likely even greater frequently). Depending on the company this system may be called:

- Career appraisal

- Performance have a look at

- Career evaluation

- Personal assessment

- Appraisal

Despite the use of diverse names, the motive of the profession appraisal device is probably similar at each enterprise agency. Your usual performance for the reason that ultimate appraisal can be evaluated towards the business enterprise's dreams, the non-public goals your manager set, and the standards considered essential on your present day project feature. The final effects of the appraisal must feed right now into the HR driven reimbursement evaluation.

As part of this technique, you will be invited to an appraisal assembly at the side of your supervisor. During this meeting, you could get to appearance his evaluation of your normal overall performance and dreams. Normally there is also a story section inside the form in which your manager can write how he feels you have got completed in the course of the one year. This will allow him to encompass topics outside of the desires that were set. This is essential because of the fact if your duties have shifted at some point of the three hundred and sixty five days then the evaluation of the desires won't be enough to truely represent your sports activities sports.

Depending at the industrial enterprise employer there can also be special sections on the form which could encompass an assessment of procedures your performance matched with the business enterprise's center values, or an assessment of your talents as compared with a preferred set of abilties expected for your role.

At the give up of the appraisal meeting, your manager will deliver an purpose of the goals that he has set you for the subsequent appraisal length. If you located his desires aren't relevant or don't truely constitute what you take delivery of as actual with you will do then this is the immediate to elevate your issues and speak the alternatives. A unique manager will welcome your input on placing your goals although he with politeness rejects your guidelines.

Not all managers, or all appraisal techniques, are the identical. You may furthermore get the opportunity to comment on the way you sense the 365 days have end up for you at any detail sooner or later of the appraisal meeting or you could handiest get one specific opportunity to talk. If the appraisal meeting isn't an open talk then I endorse you jot down any of the elements that you disagree with so that you may be brilliant to speak approximately them on the prevent of the appraisal or to encompass them in a written summary that you supply in your manager if there is no opportunity all through the assembly.

If you disagree together together with your manager's assessment of your performance then you definately honestly definately want to talk up. Many managers are very busy and that they grade humans based totally on their gut instincts. If you've got had been given been given a especially awful grade for a few issue, then ask your supervisor how he reached his cease. Review the purpose given to you using the SMART model (defincd in addition inside the "placing dreams" segment) and use it to pressure your questioning. For example, does this grade mirror a particular length that has been taken? The goal isn't to start a trouble or to show how confident you're but to get to the real thinking at the back of the grades and to get beyond any lazy control grading.

Once the appraisal assembly is over you could get the opportunity to prepare your reaction to the appraisal. This reaction might be saved as a part of the appraisal record. You will need to simply accept or reject the appraisal for the system to be whole. If you are very unhappy then you could ask your manager for every different appraisal meeting to discuss unique factors or in case you don't experience quite so strongly then you could use your decent response to feature the context which you take into account is missing.

If you find out which you cannot remedy your versions along side your manager after a second appraisal meeting and you aren't organized to signal the appraisal as it's miles, then the subsequent stage is to enlarge your troubles in your HR representative. This is a vital motion to take and consequently must handiest be performed if you sense very strongly. If you apprehend which you aren't going to win the argument then it is able to be higher to use your legit response to provide an cause of your scenario and to go away it at that.

The appraisal tool is entire when each employees member has had at the least one appraisal assembly and each the staff member and the supervisor have signed the appraisal shape.

I actually have visible many managers address the appraisal system as a waste in their time that they'll be obliged to do each 12 months. Unfortunately, this can rub-off onto their frame of workers and it's miles possible to take the mind-set that the appraisal doesn't in reality depend due to the reality my manager doesn't assume it honestly subjects. At the start of my career, I have become lucky to be warned about the importance of the appraisal way with the aid of fellow workers who had had issues with their managers at previous corporations. Their recommendation to me became that the appraisal is one of the few recorded and signed documents amongst you and your supervisor that states categorically what you in all likelihood did that 12 months and the manner well you probably did it. When issues upward thrust up then the HR branch, an internal auditor, a tribunal or a courtroom of law will take the ones files very critically. I endorse you take the identical recommendation.

To shield your self, it is a splendid idea to keep your very very own duplicate of the appraisal form and any goals that have been set that were now not entered on the shape (that is frequently the case for brand new joiners or people converting roles). Do no longer rely upon the HR crew to preserve facts and truely don't rely on any digital appraisal tool. I even have heard typically of on-line appraisal systems being upgraded and get right of access to to all preceding value determinations being out of place.

Setting desires

Your manager need to set you specific wants to acquire for the duration of your appraisal that want to be completed in advance than the subsequent profession appraisal. These goals want to be a proper away contemplated picture of what you recognize your most crucial paintings should be for the subsequent 3 hundred and sixty five days. Each purpose should be particular, measurable, SMART. Of path, this is the precept, your supervisor might not be that correct at placing SMART desires in which case you may provide an possibility phrasing for these dreams if it is going to help you.

• SMART goals are:

• Specific

• Measurable

• Assignable

• Realistic

• Time associated

During the appraisal procedure, the dreams that were previously set with the aid of your manager may be evaluated. Your average performance at every of the goals may be graded and feedback may be recorded to provide an motive of the grades.

Setting goals retroactively

The previous sections expect an remarkable worldwide wherein everybody has the right goals and that the appraisal meeting follows the ideal gadget. Unfortunately, this doesn't typically display up. Let us don't forget a few not unusual troubles.

You don't have any dreams set from a previous appraisal

Your goals don't in shape what you have got were given been asked to do this 365 days

The amazing option to each of these problems is to actively check your desires every sector to appearance if they are aligned with the art work you've got were given been doing. If they don't wholesome then speak along aspect your supervisor and ask to trade them.

If you've got been transferred from every other crew detail manner through the yr then your new supervisor need to have set your dreams even as you joined. Follow up with him if this doesn't rise up inside the first few days.

Assuming that this wasn't viable and simplest the day before your appraisal assembly you discover that the official desires which have been set for your are not applicable then the maximum in all likelihood final results is that your manager will try to define your desires retroactively at some stage within the appraisal assembly. This can be unfair due to the fact he every gadgets the goals and offers you your scores in the identical assembly with out presenting you with the danger to deliver in opposition to the modern day dreams. Also, you don't get the possibility to investigate your private solutions.

When you understand that you don't have desires set then the outstanding tactic is to write down down your very very own dreams in advance than the meeting. If you've got were given were given time then ship these dreams on your manager by manner of electronic mail earlier. Otherwise you may gift them in the course of the assembly.

During the times that your manager has no longer set desires in advance than your assembly it's far more likely to be because of the fact he's disorganized than that he has a hidden agenda to provide you a terrible appraisal. Give him the gain of the doubt. The dreams you wrote are in all likelihood to be ordinary via manner of your manager or as a minimum they will have an effect on the desires that he writes.

After the meeting, in case you feel that your appraisal become unnecessarily terrible because of the desires that he set retroactively then ask for a cutting-edge assembly to speak about your issues. Remember that the appraisal isn't always entire till you've got every given your approval to what changed into written.

Motivation - carrot and stick

In smooth terms, your employment by way of a company is a mutual agreement among you and your company. You get compensated for your time and the business corporation receives topics completed that permit it to maintain to make cash. In exercise, the agency has a huge variety of personnel from which it goals solutions and deliveries over an extended time period. These equal personnel have wonderful days and lousy days, they have got profession aspirations and most have economic pressures out of doors the place of job (domestic loans, university expenses, and so on).

The long time very last motivator of the company is that subsequent twelve months may be higher for you than this one year as long as you trust within the device and spoil the goals given to you. When you understand that there are masses of people within the commercial organization enterprise business enterprise with method roles which you would love (every in terms of hobby feature and reimbursement) then you may take delivery of as real with that what you're being presented is viable. This is the carrot the organization is dangling inside the front of you. For instance, in case you soak up extra obligation right now after a reimbursement assessment then don't expect your compensation to increase. The agency expects you to accept as proper with your corporation enough to appearance in advance to the proper time in your repayment growth.

A metaphorical "carrot" is constantly paired with a metaphorical "stick". The employer punishment "stick" is that you may lose your pastime. At the start of your profession with the organization, you can not mind an excessive amount of if you lose your manner, ultimately, you virtually landed this challenge and so why couldn't you discover a few one-of-a-kind challenge that is in reality as real? So at this degree, the concern of the "stick" might not be that plenty.

The fear of dropping your undertaking slowly creeps up on you as time is going via.

The longer you work for this business enterprise the greater effective the "stick" will become. When you have got been working there for a few years then you can have come to be in my opinion invested in that commercial enterprise enterprise. If you glide on then the goodwill investment which you have made (e.G. The network you have got were given constructed and understanding about their enterprise) is probably misplaced. Worse regardless of the reality that, you've got made a large monetary self-discipline (like shopping for a house) and also you want the monthly employment profits to hold to pay the bills. You can also have some part of your repayment (probably an advantage) paid twelve months in arrears that you can lose in case you go away.

Also, you could have been out of the challenge market for a long term with the aid of then, so your interview competencies can be rusty and you could don't have any concept how effects you could find out every unique hobby.

You can now see how worry of dropping your hobby can become a number one influencing thing for masses people at a company. Many people will though be coming to paintings to do their process notwithstanding the fact that they see no improvement on the horizon for their private situation. At this issue, the carrot now not works however the stick is probably very effective.

Prepare your self by the usage of no longer falling into this lure.

How to begin networking

It will can help you get to recognize as many people as feasible inside the corporation. Depending to your characteristic you may or may not get the hazard to satisfy with specific people at some point of the strolling day. The first humans to community with are the identical people which you paintings with every day. Building relationships with them will make it much much less tough to do your daily pastime.

Your feature may require walking with human beings out of doors of your on the spot crew once in a while. These may be humans which you need to "cross-sell" with (artwork together to promote their products) or they may be people that you will be wanting offerings or professional recommendation from. The tremendous advice is to network with the ones human beings earlier than you need their help urgently. When you need them to do something for then you it'll in all likelihood be loads smoother if you already have a outstanding dating with them.

The 1/3 desirable reason for networking is that you may be new to the enterprise and your profession route might not be in a right away line. By analyzing other people outdoor of your immediately scope of hard work you may dramatically boom the kind of feasible sideways actions in the organisation. If you're younger and ambitious then it will likely be much less complicated for a few one of a kind institution to actually receive you as a modern day senior member or as their organization leader within the occasion that they already recognise you and apprehend you. Managing people that you have by no means met earlier than may be difficult for an green supervisor.

There are many processes to network at the same time as jogging in a agency. Here are some opportunities.

• Joining human beings for coffee

• Sitting with human beings at lunch

• Town hall conferences

• Sports and cultural events

• Company barbecues

• Internal education

Coffee breaks and lunch breaks are a exquisite possibility to invite someone to join you after which to get to recognize them a touch bit higher. To entice them you may discover your self paying for his or her coffees however it will possibly be a small investment to make with a purpose to build precise relationships and to increase your community.

A Town Hall assembly is mostly a massive meeting with hundreds of humans in an auditorium. It is frequently concept of as a very one-sided conversation because the speaker talks and truely anyone else listens. Despite this, a city corridor assembly additionally can be used to growth your community. First of all, the human beings talking at the Town Hall are regularly crucial humans which you not often get to fulfill. Listen to what they are saying, and then pose questions in public inside the path of the assembly (if time is allocated for this), or ask them questions in the espresso spoil or perhaps technique them days later together with your questions. This receives you decided via them and will let you assemble relationships. Alternatively, loads of different people attend the Town Hall assembly in the target market with you. Ask them what they notion about what become stated, get to recognize them this manner.

The business enterprise might also moreover prepare sports and cultural activities. This should include a painting competition, preserving a badminton occasion, a charity run or having a football group. If you are already quite ideal at those sports sports then you may be part of the agency occasion. This is an possibility to meet human beings from precise departments that otherwise you will have no cause to satisfy with. Knowing those people might be useful at any factor in your career, you in reality don't apprehend who you can meet and the manner you'll possibly help each wonderful.

A sports activities activities and cultural event also can be a social leveling revel in. For instance, a pal of mine have turn out to be a part of the agency's soccer club and he often remarked that even senior managers got here to the soccer education durations. While they have been there they now not behaved because the boss, but as identical humans of the broader football group. This made it much less complex to approach them and to construct relationships with them.

Don't get me incorrect. I am no longer advocating becoming a member of a sports activities sports institution or getting into a marathon run just to build your community. What I am advising is that for folks who've already have been given those carrying or cultural competencies, they may be able to use those sports not only for enjoyment however moreover for reading more human beings.

The business enterprise's each 12 months barbeque or organisation picnic can be a comparable opportunity to meet humans from the broader organisation which you could not generally have the opportunity to satisfy.

Internal education publications can also offer the opportunity to meet people from fantastic factors of the enterprise employer. I in my opinion benefited from weekly language classes which enabled me to fulfill human beings whose running lifestyles couldn't had been in addition some distance from the department that I end up walking in. Learning a language together every week gave us a commonplace hobby other than work. As my profession advanced and my function grew, I met these identical humans once more however this time as paintings colleagues. Our cutting-edge friendships made it hundreds less difficult to make the number one expert contact and allowed us to artwork together with a excellent group spirit proper away. These humans remained on precise phrases with me for many years to come back once more.

During the period of human beings's careers, they're probably to change employers in some unspecified time within the destiny. There can be many human beings that you have built desirable relationships with that depart the agency even as you continue to be. When these humans go away they're likely to proportion their private email address with all of us they comprehend or invite them to be pals on some shape of social media. These connections can be very treasured and I may endorse retaining their email addresses and remaining in touch. There are some of motives for doing this.

- You will need each other hobby

- You might also need a reference

- Sharing of expert information

If you need to go away your current company then the humans you understand at particular organizations can can help you recognise what it's miles want to paintings for their commercial enterprise organization, what roles are available there and they'll even propose you to their boss. Personal suggestions built receive as true with and might "rapid song" a candidate's get admission to into a new agency.

An ex-colleague of mine moved to a first-rate competitor and some years later I done to that competitor for a assignment. I didn't realize that my friend and former colleague have become walking for the competitor. He changed into part of the senior control inside the department that I finished to. He pulled out my CV from the large quantity that had implemented and for my part recommended that they have to hire me. As a give up stop end result, I have become one of the first to be interviewed, each person that interviewed me knew that I have been advocated and they all relied on the manager that recommended me. They furnished me the technique.

Sometimes you need a referee for an software program program however you need to preserve it thriller from the humans that you artwork with. If you continue to be in touch then this is a state of affairs in which you may ask an ex-colleague to be your referee. For instance, this might be beneficial in case you observe for a technique outdoor your employer and that they need to test your references in advance than you give up.

Another precious use for particular outdoor contacts is while you need professional data from outdoor your enterprise business enterprise. For example, your commercial enterprise enterprise may also additionally ask you to make a way advice. If you have got simplest worked for this one enterprise and also you don't have plenty records of what unique groups are doing, then in advance than making the recommendation you'll probably have a private talk with an ex-colleague to recognize what their organization is doing. I am no longer suggesting that everyone shares employer secrets and strategies.

Merely which you touch the person you as quickly as labored with to get a far wider view.

When to mention "no" to extra art work

Most managers have hassle identifying their body of employees's functionality for artwork. Most often, they may definitely provide you with greater work at the same time as you end the paintings that you have already got.

At times, at the same time as the strain is on, then they'll want the enterprise to do greater artwork. When this takes region, the same old technique is in your manager to offer you more paintings than traditional on the expectation that you may stretch and locate methods to get this paintings performed. After all, surely every person within the organization is feeling the stress and so they may want you to play your element. The group stocks the weight, anyone does extra than ordinary, and the pressure reduces even as the work receives finished.

Be cautious in this case. Accepting greater artwork and handing over accurate results is super, it'll leave a protracted-lasting have an impact on in conjunction with your supervisor and alongside side your crew colleagues. Conversely, accepting greater artwork in some unspecified time within the destiny of a duration of labor strain and then not being capable of deliver may be worse than having stated no in the starting. At least if you said no then your manager may also need to have had the opportunity to bear in mind who else need to help. If it have emerge as important paintings, then your lack of delivery might be to be remembered for a long time.

Therefore, it is important to understand while to mention "no", at the same time as to mention "positive", and at the identical time as to feature threat decreasing caveats. An example is probably which you say "certain" on the know-how that in order to complete the more paintings your colleague indicates you a manner to do the challenge first.

Often the context is more complicated than the example given to this point. For instance, you can have a couple of man or woman that gives you discern to do. By stretching to deliver greater paintings for one person you will likely create battle with the alternative man or woman. In this case it is crucial to present an reason to your workload for your actual manager (the best who conducts your appraisal and approves your repayment) and allow him let you understand if the art work for the opportunity human beings can bypass ahead or no longer.

If you sense assured that you could supply, then a duration of labor stress can also additionally emerge as an possibility. Rather than equipped to receive more paintings you may volunteer to do a selected assignment which you wouldn't normally get to do and that could be useful to your career, in all likelihood a quick growth in scope or responsibility

Can I be absent from paintings?

Your company can have a insurance that permits you to be absent from paintings that may encompass the subsequent situations:

• Maternity

• Paternity

• Sickness

• Doctor's appointments

• Dentist appointments

- Holiday/holiday

- Bereavement

Your organisation's business organisation agency manual or internal net site will provide an explanation for the hints spherical those one-of-a-type reasons for absence. What it will not provide an reason for is the social popularity or the expectation of your colleagues in the direction of whether or not or no longer or now not those absences are taken or now not.

When a woman is pregnant then she is probable to make entire use of the maternity coverage offered via her organisation. There will though be some girls who depart early and others who don't go away till the day they pass into medical institution, however this appears to be determined more via using the hazard to the kid and the mother's fitness than any social expectation. I actually have never heard of everyone being pressured to take plenty much less than the overall maternity depart.

More and more corporations now moreover offer the fathers of latest baby kids a quick duration of absence. My personal experience is that fathers generally take this benefit if it's far supplied, but, they will be advocated when they take it each by manner of their own family and via way in their cutting-edge state of affairs at paintings. For example, I actually have said new fathers who've been not in a role to stop what they have been doing for two weeks and as a end end result, instead, they took a loss of days normal with week for some of weeks to help their spouse with the contemporary little one.

Sickness is a far extra complex venture. There are generally kinds of infection benefits which are supplied depending on the corporation. One shape of insurance offers a difficult and fast extensive form of days consistent with yr that may be used for sickness and on the equal time as these days are used up then the employee want to apply their tour/excursion days inside the occasion that they want to increase their absence. The special kind of coverage is to offer an almost limitless quantity of unwell days with certain regulations.

My experience is that companies that provide a set quantity of ill days consistent with yr discover that their employees make entire use of all of the days supplied. That is to say that, the days are visible as a unique form of emergency tour via the employee that can be used for added than illness. These days are continuously taken at quick word (as actual infection might be) and as a quit result, can be quite disruptive. I would likely furthermore risk a wager that personnel with a hard and speedy allocation of ill days grow to be taking extra days off on commonplace than people with endless unwell days. The top information is that taking all the days internal your sick day allocation is socially perfect and I actually have not visible it getting used as a each yr appraisal metric.

An countless ill day coverage is pretty special. The form of days may be theoretically unlimited but the controls around the use of in recent times are lots tighter. For instance, inner a effective sort of days of absence, the worker ought to go to a clinical doctor and get a systematic certificate to show that he's unable to attend art work. Then if he is nevertheless absent after a few other few weeks then the worker may be invited to go to the enterprise corporation clinical medical doctor who will determine, on behalf of the enterprise, whether or now not or no longer this person is genuinely healthful for paintings or not.

It is certainly socially perfect for humans with unlimited ill days to have some absences in keeping with twelve months of a few days at a time or to have a whole week's absence eventually. However, the full form of days taken is likely to be quite low on common besides the employee has a essential contamination or attends sanatorium for a surgery. Many people can be proud that they've not been absent due to sickness for an prolonged time frame.

The awful information with the endless unwell day policy is that the quantity of days taken each one year is probably to have a function to play to your overall performance appraisal and to your compensation assessment. For example, if someone has had extra than 2 weeks' absence due to infection at the same time as you take into account that their very last appraisal then they will be in all likelihood to have this point written of their new appraisal and they may need to offer an reason for the situation in their appraisal assembly. Also if the organization gives standard overall performance-associated bonuses then it is probably that the bonus might be decreased (prorated) with the resource of the giant kind of days absent.

Of course, there might be times at the same time as you could't assist your self and you may need to take days off unwell. The cause of this section is really to make you aware of the results.

Keeping in shape and healthful can lessen the kind of sick days which you need to take. To help you with this, many corporates will offer get right of entry to to a health club, or perhaps each 365 days fitness checks. Find out which opportunities are to be had to you.

Holiday or excursion allowances can also be for steady numbers of days in line with 12 months or, in some times, unlimited days. My enjoy is that endless vacation allowances are not often indulged in really through personnel. These forms of allowance are commonly exceptional supplied while there's already a sturdy social satisfaction in no longer taking hundreds day off, as a end result having endless holidays is purely theoretical due to the fact no-one gets to take prolonged holidays within the ones corporates with out unfavourable their career.

Be aware that during some corporates you need to accrue days before you can take them as a holiday. Therefore, while you start working for this type of enterprise you've got 0 days excursion in your tour account. After three months you may accrue one-1/3 of your annual holiday balance and so on. As a stop end result, in case you have become married on your first yr of employment then your absence need to be negotiated with them in advance than your be a part of.

What training is to be had to me?

A important company can also moreover have its non-public training branch with its private catalog of available training. This may be a part of the corporation itself or outsourced to a third birthday party. It is probable to provide the following schooling.

• Business training

• Sales

• Public speaking

• Office gear

• Efficiency schooling

• Management

- Career price determinations

- Project manage

- Languages

- Graduate schooling

- Fast tune schooling

- Mandatory schooling

Business training will cowl any schooling for the priority vicinity of the center enterprise agency that the business enterprise is engaged in. There is probably get entry to-stage education at the manner to be open to each worker and greater superior education that would handiest be available to human beings in sales-producing roles.

Almost each employer sells some factor to external customers, whether or not or no longer or no longer this is products or services of a few kind. Normally handiest the salespeople might be eligible to attend the commercial agency organization's profits training courses.

Public speaking courses may be outstanding and varied. Some will provide interest to a manner to make a presentation to a small target audience and others can be extra specialized in conjunction with how to speak to the out of doors media. The access-diploma guides can be available to in reality anybody, and the more specialized publications may be limited to humans whose roles genuinely require this schooling.

Training on administrative center equipment can be open to everyone. This includes training on spreadsheets, phrase processing, e-mail gear, and so on.

Efficiency education may be open to every body and could encompass subjects on the facet of time control, or managing meetings.

Management education is in all likelihood to be furnished at many distinct tiers. There may be a smooth control path for emblem spanking new organization leaders. Then there can be a multi-session path over a duration of some months for added senior control. In addition, there is probably some of professional manipulate publications.

The HR branch will probably run a route on how to put together for and conduct career fee determinations. In a few groups, this could be obligatory for surely absolutely everyone that has to behavior fee determinations.

Project manipulate publications are in all likelihood to be supplied to anyone turning into a venture manager or who has first rate venture manipulate content material internal their role.

Some multinational agencies also can furthermore offer overseas language commands. Usually, the correct languages decided on are vital to the business enterprise which consist of being the language used in their head administrative center or of their critical remote places subsidiaries.

Graduate training may be compulsory for all entrants on the graduate training software.

Eligible senior personnel can be invited to join a representative fast music education software program that is designed to put together human beings to grow to be the excessive fliers of the company employer.

In addition, there may be a number of obligatory education instructions that personnel need to wait in the course of the one year just so the company can meet its regulatory desires. These need to embody anti-coins laundering, anti-corruption, information privateness, and fitness and safety schooling publications.

You can have visible that some of the ones training courses are extraordinary open to humans in fantastic roles, and one of a kind guides are open to anyone who desires to beautify their skills. Within your first years within the enterprise business enterprise, you may want to gain from as many guides as feasible that will help you become higher at your method and to in the end make progress to your career. So one of the key questions is how an awful lot education are you allowed to have and what sort of education is socially suitable inside your corporation or department.

Your manager will preserve a training finances. Before the last economic crisis, those education budgets have been pretty large and regularly they did now not get genuinely spent from three hundred and sixty five days to 365 days. Since the financial disaster, many managers can have a much smaller training finances or maybe no price range in any respect. Despite this, there's nevertheless an employee expectation that they need to get keep of education. For instance, I can remember many humans through the years who have advised me that they expect to get hold of schooling possibilities in line with twelve months. I don't anticipate I ever saw this written down everywhere but many humans shared this same notion.

My advice is that the right schooling may be an remarkable factor and can surely allow you to do your current-day pastime and to development. I would propose that you get to recognize the training coverage of your business enterprise and test the courses on provide thru manner of the training department. Within your first few years at the organisation, if you apprehend that your characteristic makes you eligible for effective training publications then I propose you have a look at for them immediately or at least you talk them at the side of your manager and make him conscious which you need them. These professional guides are supplied for a purpose so don't leave it to hazard that your manager makes the connection himself.

If you enjoy that they could benefit you, and you are not overbooked with distinctiveness training guides, then I would suggest that you look at for a number of the open-get proper of access to courses too (e.G. Public speaking or place of job device). Your supervisor will need to approve all of your training guides and he goes to genuinely will let you apprehend if he thinks that you are asking for an excessive amount of. Make it easy on your supervisor that via letting you attend those courses you will be extra green in a while so the investment in money and time may be absolutely really worth it.

Unfortunately, it is possible to fall into the lure of now not attending any training courses for years on prevent. This can appear on the same time as you're very committed on your work, you understand the place you are in has a immoderate workload and likely your supervisor has made it clean that he wishes the team inside the office for as many hours as possible. You can also additionally get quick time period advantages from this approach, e.G. An outstanding appraisal and standard performance bonus, but once it will become normal then no-one will experience that you are creating a sacrifice anymore and you can not be getting both the recognition or the schooling.

Knowing extra about compensation

At some thing, you'll want to comprehend what precise humans are being paid. Unfortunately, many agencies say that discussing your earnings with other personnel will result in instant termination of employment. This is difficult because of the truth in case you don't realize what your colleagues are being paid then how do in case you are being paid quite, and if you don't apprehend what your manager is being paid then how do you recognise what you can intention for?

Some personnel will talk their repayment with paintings colleagues that they accept as true with that they're able to bear in mind. This could likely art work for them, but they may be taking the chance that the facts isn't always the whole fact. A colleague might also additionally tell them a lower determine to avoid a complaint that might be traced again to them. Or a colleague may moreover country a better discern definitely to create jealousy.

Alternatively, you can each ask a nice recruitment consultant or look for unbiased data on a net web page which include GlassDoor. The recruitment consultant will recognize very well the salaries for human beings he has located but might not apprehend the reimbursement for every characteristic. GlassDoor is more impartial, however it's miles worth sorting out a number of their facts in your enterprise earlier than you actually take delivery of as real with it.

Regular reorganizations

Corporates, in particular the famous ones with plenty of shareholders, don't usually generally tend to face nonetheless for pretty lengthy. You can count on that every 5 years there may be a high change.

• The purpose for a splendid alternate might be:

• Profits are down and price-cutting is wanted

• The enterprise enters new business enterprise traces

• The enterprise exits vintage commercial employer traces

• There is a exchange in pinnacle manage

• Responding to reorganization a few location else

In the reorganization, there might be winners and losers. Even even as the reorganization is added on by means of boom it is even though viable that a few human beings will lose their jobs or be forced to simply accept an awful lot much less attractive roles in the occasion that they need to live. While at the identical time, a few human beings also can gain more interesting roles or acquire a merchandising.

Unless the reorganization is dictated in element from the top control then it's miles in all likelihood that strolling committees may be created to help format the current day business business enterprise or to choose out out feasible improvements. The individuals who are invited to take part in those committees will want to find out the time further to their everyday responsibilities (don't assume any help), but at the same time, they have got the possibility to construct relationships with other departments and to study in-intensity how precise business traces paintings. Furthermore, only the first-rate humans are picked for those committees and consequently they will understand that senior manipulate is aware about them actually thru manner of one among a type characteristic of being decided on.

If you aren't decided on to be in one of the committees then the high-quality you could do is to attempt to discover from your colleagues what's being discussed. Knowing the in all likelihood outcome of the reorganization can also furthermore help you function yourself as an employee that definitely ought to be in a key function interior one of the new agencies.

Surviving mergers and acquisitions

Corporations are in all likelihood to merge with awesome organizations or to be acquired with the useful resource of them apparently with none warning. In exercise, the pinnacle control will understand complete properly if they may be making plans a merger and they'll be having talks with the other organisation for months earlier than they inform anyone of their own enterprise. I suspect they'll furthermore have a few idea of being a functionality acquisition target earlier than it is stated openly.

Mergers and acquisitions may be very traumatic times for employees. In the start, very little records may be available and also you obtained't recognize whether or no longer your process may be without delay affected or now not.

The first time a business agency that I became working for emerge as worried in a merger, pals outdoor had been telling me that I would check greater about what have turn out to be going on from outside news offerings than I might awaiting inner business enterprise announcements. I idea this become a shaggy canine story till I observed out that they had been right.

Reading the facts to find out what's taking location in the course of a merger may be a ways more informative than looking in advance on your personal commercial enterprise agency to make an internal announcement. My simplest concept as to why it appears this way is that the information offerings are organized to place up rumors that they have obtained from properly property, even as your company can't threat telling you some component till it's been agreed to formally through the usage of all occasions. This can cause quite a cast off in conversation.

There are severa possible affects on your function because of the fact the result of a merger or foremost acquisition. These have to embody.

• Redundancy

• Joining a bigger organization

• Changing roles

- Working in a smaller institution

- No impact in any respect

In the extreme case, you could lose your interest through redundancy after a merger or acquisition. If the ultra-present day business employer has publicly added that it's miles going to reduce staff numbers as a price-reducing diploma then you definately truly honestly understand that redundancy for some human beings goes to seem. At this diploma, I ought to propose searching out out extra about wherein the redundancies are likely to take area. For example, this may show up in overlapping commercial commercial enterprise business enterprise regions or in regions wherein the modern agency has no cause of persevering with.

The merger or acquisition can also additionally boom the size of your branch and you can discover yourself walking in a larger crew. This will create opportunities for some humans to control those large businesses however it could moreover propose that a few managers get moved sideways within the occasion that they don't get requested to run the today's groups.

Long earlier than there is any talk about redundancies, you'll be requested to sign up for a state-of-the-art team with a ultra-modern feature. If you are being certainly invited to do that based on gain then this could be a remarkable pass.

It is likewise viable that the branch or group which you art work in may be shrunk and you could be provided a position in the decreased agency. Again this can create possibilities for a few humans and sideways actions for others. For instance, in reducing the current group a few people can be moved out and this can leave interesting roles open for current group individuals to fill.

Not all managers are progressive. Your new supervisor may also additionally have determined to your new feature with out wondering very difficult about your capabilities or how the change will have an effect on you. If you are sad then speak to your supervisor. Better even though, research an opportunity in advance than speaking in your supervisor. Then he is going to see you assisting him, thru supplying an answer, in area of without a doubt complaining which you are not satisfied.

Revenue generating roles are plenty less in all likelihood to be permit pass in a downturn. These are the jobs that right now make cash for the company (e.G. Income positions). The exception to this can be in a merger of equals at the identical time as competing businesses of comparable period merge. The purpose may be to lessen walking expenses and, as a result, there can be much less roles wanted or perhaps profits generating roles are at hazard.

As an instance of what can appear while you ask, a chum of mine turned into going for walks for a agency in New York City on the identical time as it turned into abruptly acquired with the useful resource of a competitor. His new supervisor proposed him a strong however dull feature. There have been no exceptional roles. Then, via the usage of talking up my buddy acquired a awesome severance bundle deal and became able to begin a new profession in Paris, France.

You can also discover that there may be no effect the least bit to your cutting-edge feature and responsibilities. This should nicely be the case if the enterprise region you are in is seen as complementary to the alternative employer, wherein case that branch or organization will maintain as it is and turns into growing through the years.

A colleague of mine come to be now not snug with the uncertainty of the merger scenario his employer commercial enterprise company had entered into. So he started out actively searching out jobs together together with his corporation's opposition. During one of his subsequent interviews, one of the interviewing managers shared a few recommendation with him it is definitely worth repeating right proper right here. He stated that he had been via many mergers and located them a amazing deal an awful lot much less volatile than converting employers. It takes years to construct a high-quality popularity and to be diagnosed, many people from the modern-day-day employer will live after the merger and you may however have that community.

Moving to a ultra-modern business organization way starting all over again. My colleague took this advice and observed the merger thru.

Imagine if you have been one step in advance of the merger? This is possible in case you be part of a merger challenge pressure. Senior managers will make the large options about employer corporation shape and headcount numbers publish merger but they'll depart the information of the group systems to the department heads and corporation line heads. These humans are likely to invite modern-day employees to work inside the merger mission stress to take a look at the two companies and make targeted proposals for branch systems after the merger. You may be requested to sign up for a assignment stress or there can be possibilities to volunteer to join. Bcing invited to the undertaking pressure is often a correct signal that your competencies are diagnosed and that you may be retained.

Joining a merger assignment pressure is lots of more paintings, but you could have an massive records advantage over your colleagues that might despite the fact that be ready to listen what's going to take vicinity to them.

Raising issues collectively collectively along with your manager

There are many motives why you could need to raise issues together along with your manager, these embody:

• You have issues with some other group member

• You have problems at the side of your supervisor

• You have troubles with wonderful organizations

- Issues collectively with your compensation

All parents can be in this situation once in a while. Therefore, the fantastic manner to technique it's miles to hook up with your manager and construct a relationship earlier than you want his help. Then, on the equal time as you ask for a assembly he's going to offer you with the time and on the same time as you start speaking he is aware of that he can speak to you and he will pay attention. If the primary real contact you have collectively along side your manager is while you raise an problem to him then you definitely are already at the over again-foot.

Even if you don't have a longtime connection, you could nevertheless don't forget asking your manager if he would like to sign up for you for a espresso or to have lunch with you. That gives you the possibility to bring together the very starting of a dating earlier than launching into your problems. Then in the direction of the espresso or lunch begin to open up about your trouble. Also, this technique takes the brink of an hassle through making it less formal so it is probably suitable for discussing humans or undertaking problems however there are times while a more formal assembly is probably better (e.G. You would like to surrender).

When you do contact your manager with an trouble then study the issue first. Certainly don't have this communication while you are angry approximately what truely occurred and also you simply want your manager to pay interest, he is not there for that.

Try to approach your supervisor with answers now not virtually troubles. For instance, we're having a trouble with X and to clear up this I propose we do Y or Z for the ones motives. In this way you are making it masses much much less complex for him to determine (you've got were given finished the analysis) and he is going to recollect which you are someone who comes with solutions not without a doubt problems.

This approach will paintings well in an open and green paintings environment, if this isn't always the case or there are mitigating times then don't forget a greater formal technique, together with elevating a complaint as defined in the next segment.

Hard fact approximately raising grievances

If you have had been given a problem with some other member of your team who's at the same stage as you, then if you could't clear up your variations the subsequent direction of motion can be to increase the problem for your manager. Or in case you are having issues collectively along with your manager then your subsequent step is to prepare a selected one on one meeting with him.

By this degree you need to preserve your very very personal private written record of what takes region; embody dates, instances, key human beings and what have become stated. Print essential emails in your data. If the state of affairs changed into to blow-up and a 3rd birthday party involves audit the state of affairs then you definitely want to expose proof of what has already taken vicinity.

At this degree, the problem can be resolved short thru speakme on your supervisor. If not, and you experience that you can't put up with it to any amount further then you will need to increase the problem nonetheless similarly and take it to your HR representative. Their first approach may be to try to clear up the problem informally many of the HR representative and all of the sports involved.

Maybe you experience that you are in a specially bad situation and that there may be no price in in search of to treatment a hassle informally then you can cross immediately in your HR consultant and raise an legitimate criticism. This will then be regarded into with the resource of your HR consultant. It can be recorded in your HR report which you raised this criticism and what the final results of it changed into.

A grievance isn't always some thing to be entered into lightly. It is most customarily used by a person who feels that their problems are so fantastic that they'll no longer be able to keep going for walks for that employer if their troubles aren't resolved. Only growth a criticism even as you revel in that raising a complaint to HR obtained't be enough. Frequently this route is taken even as the employees' hassle is with their line manager.

To recognize how the complaint method is finished we want to first appearance more deeply at the function of the Human Resource Department (HR). The HR group may be contacted for all manner of personnel-related troubles. Before drawing near them with our troubles we need to undergo in thoughts very carefully how they'll react and whose issue they'll be on. Will they behave independently, will they protect the employee or will they take the enterprise agency line?

There is an vintage saying amongst personnel that the HR department's actual purpose is to shield the organization from its employees. This is visible thru some humans as being a terrible announcement approximately the HR department. Personally, I discover it quite a realistic way of looking on the state of affairs and I will give an motive behind why.

Let us have a look at the alternatives first. Many human beings do not forget that HR is without a doubt impartial and sincere. I am nice that a number of them would really like to be, however it isn't going to be viable whilst their wages are paid thru the organization they paintings for now not the personnel. Furthermore, they need to have a close to jogging courting with the senior managers to whom they may be assigned as their HR partners. They will now not be rewarded for being altruistic. So there is little threat of them being clearly impartial.

However, imagine if a criticism turn out to be raised in the direction of the same manager that they want to have a near walking dating with. What if simple evidence arises throughout the complaint technique that there is a actual problem with the supervisor to whom the complaint come to be raised closer to and the problem may want to go to a court docket of law or an employment tribunal. In this case, there can be a point at which the HR group will must stop supporting the supervisor in question. They may not prevent helping him because of the truth they are independent, we have got got already removed that choice, but due to the reality their situation might in all likelihood then be how they'll shield the enterprise from the rogue manager and the manner they will limit the effect of the criticism that could now be upheld.

In stop, if you need a conflict resolved then you may need to raise it on your HR consultant. This is a manner. In the start, your complaint may be heard with an unbiased thoughts-set, however because of the reality the criticism proceeds expect the HR organization to facet together with your supervisor. Later on, in case your grievance looks like it is going to be upheld then it will achieve the point that the organization needs to be blanketed on the price of the supervisor and the HR team may additionally additionally appear to be in your aspect once more.

Whistle blowing

One unique war choice alternative is a whistle-blowing movement. This cannot be used for average overall performance-related issues or elevating problems approximately your direct supervisor. It is used to tell on an movement that befell that have turn out to be no longer within the business organisation's interest and from which the character elevating the grievance desires to be included. For instance, if one worker sees every other employee cheating a purchaser then he may moreover need to complain using the whistle-blowing device. If he grow to be wrong and there was no harm finished to the client then he can also want to not be penalized for making the complaint due to the fact he need to have been covered by means of way of the manner.

The purpose of the method is to allow employees to elevate their worries approximately conditions that would in any other case damage the business enterprise and to experience that they're loose to speak without a repercussions.

How being mentored can help you

Many humans benefit from having a mentor to help them with their profession. Most CEOs and heads of commercial enterprise enterprise will have been mentored sooner or later in their career.

Typically a mentor is an unbiased character who isn't a part of your direct manage line but is more professional than you. The concept is that you could discuss what's occurring on your profession with this man or woman and set dreams for what you need to seem. The mentor can then help you evaluate whether or not or not or no longer you're going in the proper route to meet your desires and to help you offer you with techniques to achieve it. You will be expected to do the paintings and the mentor is there that will help you gain it.

Some groups have inner mentoring programs. Their HR departments can also additionally even fit mentors to mentees. They are possibly to aim individuals who, with a few assistance, need to make it onto the control fast tune.

If you observed that this is some difficulty that you could gain from however your agency does no longer offer this shape of software then you may although search for a person internally who may want to help you on a voluntary foundation or you can look for a mentor outdoor the corporation. Some external mentors will expect to be paid and others will assist you for no longer anything as they will had been helped in this way at some point of their career.

Increasing your cost to the commercial enterprise enterprise

If you would really like to have an extended and rich career interior your current corporation corporation then you definitely definately certainly want to take a look at the rate you offer them in recent times and what you can do to boom your charge. Having a more fee in evaluation for your pals need to assist you advantage opportunities for career development and no a great deal much less than ought to make certain you maintain your technique throughout times of difficulty while one of a type people are losing theirs.

These are some examples of factors you may do to growth your charge.

• International venture

• Secondment to a few other branch

• Business training

• Management schooling

• Become a mentor

• Learn a language

• Join an business organization corporation

Having been on an global experience you may be extra valuable to the employer because of the truth you could comprehend how the organization operates in multiple region inside the international. You could have furthermore received useful contacts in that area. A a success worldwide undertaking demonstrates to senior manipulate that you are bendy and will be taken into consideration once more for some different assignment.

I can reflect onconsideration on examples of many people who after they have started having global assignments they selected to preserve to art work remote places in awesome roles for the relaxation in their careers. I apprehend of different examples in which pals had a series of assignments remote places interspersed with durations decrease lower back at headquarters in-among assignments.

A friend as speedy as defined to me that he labored for a Scandinavian multinational company. He had labored for them in a unmarried u . S . But changed into no longer being furnished the worldwide roles that he desired. He started out out to research the language of the headquarters and shortly after have become supplied a secondment to the headquarters. Once he had spent 3 years on the center of the organization then he knew the crucial component humans and understood very well the manner of life and values of the corporation. Soon after he commenced to be presented the global roles that he sought.

A similar increase in price may be accomplished by using converting departments. Global organizations can also perform in enterprise line silos however they may moreover realise the significance of getting a few humans who've worked in multiple region. Therefore if the possibility arises, a person can upload rate with the useful useful resource of running in a remarkable location for some time. This may be visible as a sideways pass in the quick term however in the long time, it may definitely help in obtaining a senior manage position.

Knowing greater about the company's center commercial organisation will increase your fee. I ought to indicate learning as plenty as viable from the human beings round you, from any internal customers you could have and from taking any enterprise business enterprise education guides which might be supplied. This is a want if you art work in a sales-producing position, however it's also of amazing price in case you are in a beneficial aid function. The key people in any guide characteristic need to have a deep statistics of the actual business employer of the enterprise employer, no longer truly statistics in their assist region. When assist capabilities are being offshored or outsourced, then having right corporation expertise may be seen as a big advantage. Remember that the expertise of the commercial corporation is one expertise that outside outsourced body of workers will not be capable of provide.

Good managers are valued in any enterprise organization. If you have were given got aspirations within the route of a control career route then take every opportunity to come to be a higher manager. One way of doing this is to attend any control schooling publications that you are entitled to. Another method is probably to attend any control associated talks that the organisation organizes. For instance, in case you meant to be a challenge supervisor then taking note of venture managers from the improvement enterprise who've controlled massive building tasks can be inspirational. Also, you could be a part of an industry control body out of doors of work in which like-minded human beings get together and percent their studies.

If there may be an expert internal mentoring application then you could volunteer to end up a mentor. This would possibly permit you to meet people outside of your private on the spot area. Also helping distinctive humans in this way is probably that will help you to sharpen your very personal abilities. Because it's miles the proper inner mentor software then HR and senior manipulate will understand that you are helping other employees, so your effort ought to get popularity as properly.

Global organizations, with the resource of definition, perform in many nations. Even if English is the common language of the agency the nearby businesses in every usa will despite the fact that speak their neighborhood language amongst themselves. Furthermore, if the headquarters of the global corporation isn't always in an English speakme u.S. Of the usa of the usa then the business enterprise can also have that language as a vital language. Learning this language may be the key to building relationships with people at the headquarters. It can also motive a secondment to the headquarters which can be an terrific long term profession go together with the float.

For a number of years in my profession, I made a every day try and test the language of the headquarters. It enabled me to take roles at the headquarters wherein I managed groups who have been no longer sturdy in English. As I advanced in each my profession and my language skills, I changed into invited to meetings wherein no English modified into spoken and I ran guidance committees with out speaking English. Looking over again on it, each member of the guidance committee also can want to talk English well and once I met with them one to at the least one they often decided on to speak English, however when they have been all collectively in a room then they desired to talk in their private language. I can not say that I could have been barred from any of those roles if I couldn't speak their language, but I am certain that thru speakme their language a degree of self perception and remember modified into constructed which helped my profession.

The downside of analyzing a language is that it takes pretty a few strength and staying energy over a duration of a few years. Therefore, you need to maintain in thoughts if that may be a sensible investment or whether or not or not you'll be better spending time on greater industrial employer training or extra manipulate schooling. The language itself may not be a transferable capability if you skip to some other business enterprise that does not use that language, but, reading a 2nd language is also gaining the abilties to research in addition new languages. It is a non-public choice.

It may also be of fee in case you joined an organisation agency. An ex-colleague of mine modified into an professional in a particular shape of banking verbal exchange technology. He volunteered to be the organisation's consultant on the bypass-organisation committee to speak about the use and development of this era. It became some thing he desired to do and it brought charge to him and to the agency.

Remember that ultimately everything is set profits. The commercial enterprise organization you figure for wishes to make sales to exist. Everyone within the organisation must preserve this in mind, it isn't a subject handiest for income-humans. The most valuable matters you could do will each defend the organization's income (e.G. Regulatory safety) or without delay help the organization to get more clients, then promote more products and services. Therefore, if faced with options, constantly pick out out the one that is the most intently aligned with profits.

How workplace politics can have an effect on you

Office politics is a electricity play wherein a group of human beings within the workplace use their function to advantage some advantage that is regularly detrimental to the interests of the business enterprise agency as a whole.

In any massive group of humans, a few form of politics is in all likelihood to take region. So place of job politics has its roots in everyday human organization conduct. How it differs in big corporates is that the capacity rewards for a a success energy play might be very attractive.

The preferred final consequences from office politics may moreover embody:

- Looking after their pals

- Currying want with the department head

- Self-advertising and marketing

- Reinforcing organization contention

In the super case, you can see administrative center politics as no extra than favoritism. Perhaps there can be an corporation event that everyone would like to head on. Then you discover that the least deserving individual has been invited but he often has coffee in a group at the side of your manager's boss and so your supervisor decided on him to delight his boss. This is a minor case of place of work politics, it could have an impact on the inducement of the group but no actual damage is executed.

Often place of business politics has the intention to restrict rival corporations. Imagine that groups have unique scope but they want to paintings together on some topics which will get their paintings finished. When there may be political competition, one organisation may additionally additionally avoid co-running with the possibility team. This cooperation might be to be based mostly on goodwill and simply so they dispose of all goodwill. Typical conditions encompass refusing to react to urgent requests and locating petty reasons to reject requests for cooperation. In public, they will, of course, declare to be cooperating and following the rules. Usually, this has no extra value than to hold the opposition going.

When workplace politics grow to be poisonous

When workplace politics are taken to extra then the place of work is regularly described as having emerge as a poisonous political surroundings.

The rewards sought by using the ones assignment toxic politics can also embody:

• Keeping their jobs

• Gaining give up of one year bonuses

• Removing different personnel that might divulge them

• Promoting human beings from their internal circle

• Influencing alternatives

Those spending excessive quantities of time on place of business politics may be failing in their real obligations of employment. They may also moreover have some element to cowl. They acquire as actual with that by means of the use of way of manipulating or threatening distinct employees, that they may no longer tell the entire truth to senior control and so as to be sufficient to keep the repute quo. As a give up result, they will maintain their jobs and affect. Instead, if the reality have become to come out they may find out themselves on a performance evaluate or in all likelihood be sacked.

To reap this manipulation they may be probable to inform lies and create fake rumors about the people that they want to control. With their gift have an effect on, they rely upon being believed extra than the individual that is being manipulated.

In a similar way, the supervisor of a politically poisonous group may additionally moreover make over-exaggerated claims approximately the employer's everyday performance that three hundred and sixty five days believing that it will bring about higher reimbursement for him and his group. The trouble with this is that corporates frequently have very interconnected teams and so with the beneficial resource of their claiming how nicely they've finished it's far probably to intend that each exclusive group ought to have completed badly and risks receiving lots lots less repayment than they deserve.

This electricity play is also probable to depend upon telling lies to senior manage and having those lies believed. As this is aimed closer to discrediting a whole organization then this is extra audacious than discrediting one individual and is possibly to require a marketing campaign over a duration of months to tarnish the recognition of the alternative organization.

A lots much less tough manipulation for a supervisor who's engaged in poisonous politics is to have one person removed that otherwise dangers exposing him and his inner circle. At a junior diploma, they may virtually find "dirt" on the person that underneath normal conditions have to advantage no extra than a verbal warning, but in this example, they may train HR to location the man or woman on widespread performance evaluation after which manipulate him out of the organization (quasi legally).

An opportunity is to (incorrectly) grade a person very badly in an decent profession appraisal. After which the identical common common performance overview technique may be located. If the character centered doesn't have a strong voice inside the company and doesn't have any influential friends then the electricity play is probably quite smooth for them to accumulate.

If the toxic supervisor's crew is greater than his private internal circle then he received't be able to resist "searching after" his internal circle to the detriment of diverse human beings within the group. He can promote truely everybody he needs inner his organization without any due system if he feels that it'll advantage his cause. The folks which are passed over for advertising and marketing internal his wider group can super complain to HR, they will be now not going to have sufficient have an effect on for it to be clearly absolutely well worth elevating the difficulty out of doors the broader crew and certainly not with the toxic manager. Unfortunately, if the poisonous supervisor has a sturdy voice then HR will take delivery of his opinion over the courtroom docket times of his wider team.

Another electricity play from the poisonous supervisor may be to steer a number one choice a very good manner to gain some advantage for him and his inner circle. For instance, a take a look at may be finished to pick out among outside providers. The poisonous supervisor and his internal circle may additionally use their have an impact on to make certain that their preferred provider is chosen. They also can then advantage with the resource of gaining some control over the company relationship or claiming credit score score for the deliveries of the outside provider. The supplier will no longer contradict them because of the reality they'll have understood that they were best decided on due to the have an impact on of the poisonous manager.

The identical poisonous manager may also pick out out to pay the team of workers that he favors extra than his other personnel. This generally way that he's going to skew the reimbursement assessment in the route of those in his internal circle or inside the direction of various people after which he's going to gain have an impact on over them. This isn't always the behavior of a meritocracy. Up and coming stars that might mission the poisonous manager inside the destiny might not be compensated quite.

During an internal audit, someone within the company is requested to test a particular vicinity of hobby in the enterprise to grade the overall performance of the hobby and to make guidelines. An audit of this kind is also open to place of job politics. Someone with have an effect on can manage the people conducting the audit to decide the very last outcomes. Possible motivations for manipulating the final consequences of the audit consist of discrediting the humans being audited or hiding evidence in opposition to their inner circle. Clearly, this manipulation of an audit wouldn't advantage the enterprise agency in any manner.

So how can you navigate your manner through the wallet of toxic politics and get on together with your very non-public profession? First of all, you want to be conscious and be conscious while the sort of situations is beginning (see the tick list in the subsequent segment). Addressing it, later on may be more tough (especially in case your popularity has already been broken). I should suggest keeping data of what's stated that has the danger of turning toxic and amassing any evidence you may. Regarding your non-public standard overall performance, accumulate comments from the humans which you are turning in to. Also, this is in which your non-public personal network becomes treasured, you could want those who can corroborate your model of sports.

One different shape of protection may be to talk your very own successes extra often. It is difficult to assault a person's recognition if all of us is aware of that you are someone who offers.

Escalating those toxic conditions to HR is not probable to advantage you. Those playing politics are usually clever sufficient to carry out within the grey areas in which there may be no actual reality, surely one individual's word in opposition to each different. Remember that a poisonous supervisor who's greater senior than you is possibly to have greater effect over HR than you.

By now you will be questioning that during case you ever locate your self on this kind of conditions then you definately virtually really might be better off joining them as opposed to looking to artwork spherical them. I may also endorse within the direction of it. To begin with, it is probably to take years of complete subservience to be preferred into the internal circle of a set of human beings like this. Secondly, and more importantly, in case you charge openness, honesty, and meritocracy then you can find out it difficult to place apart your values to act inside the manner that they might want. You also can console yourself with the query of techniques well those humans might possibly continue to exist in the event that they had to find out a hobby outside in a brand new business agency in which they could now not have the protection of their toxic politics.

When you lose out because of office politics, then take the time to remind yourself how desirable you're. You may moreover furthermore were rejected for the advertising and advertising and marketing that you preferred, or you have were given had your paintings criticized, but if it is because of toxic place of work politics, then you could recognize that you pleasant were given stuck in the crossfire. It is vital to preserve yourself belief and understand that without politics, you'll be extremely good manipulate together with your competencies. It is great a quick hiccup in your prolonged career. Instead of dwelling on the bias, make plans for the destiny.

Toxic office politics tick list

If you have got issues which you are coming into a poisonous paintings environment then try the tick list below.

• Your manager has an internal circle that doesn't in shape crew hierarchy.

• This inner circle meets frequently and for lengthy periods.

• Your manager avoids committing to a few aspect in writing.

• People outside the circle get terrible cost determinations.

• People outdoor the circle get handed over often.

• No cooperation with organizations out of doors.

• Speaking by myself with senior control is unlawful.

• Unexplained redundancies.

- Good performers on "closing threat" development packages.

- High body of employees turnover outside the circle.

- No team of workers turnover in the circle.

- Speaking up is frowned upon.

- Important employer records is not shared.

- Your supervisor isn't trusted by the usage of the usage of one in all a kind groups.

- The agency rule ebook doesn't appear to apply.

- Praise out of doors the circle is unusual.

- Positive comments from clients now not shared.

- No possibility to present feedback.

- Never invited to way evaluate workshops.

- Manager is at battle with tremendous departments.

- No 2d possibilities outside the circle.

- Culture of worry.

You can also additionally have a toxicity problem inside the administrative center if a significant amount of these checks are best.

Crossing the Rubicon to control

Get identified as a supervisor

If you have already taken the selection that you would possibly choose your career to transport inside the route of coping with, then to make that float you want to be identified on your manage capabilities earlier than gaining your first opportunity to be a supervisor.

After you have got got declared your hobby on top of factors then senior control might be looking for to look if you display the right capabilities for them to take the hazard of providing you with a control feature. These abilties should embody:

• Amicable relationships with distinctive employees

• Good communique talents

• Sharing your facts and supporting special institution human beings

• Supporting the management line (now not being a rebellion)

• Adding price in your modern manager

• Being curious approximately the bigger picture

• Having self guarantee

However, watching any of these behaviors will art work in opposition to you:

- Being overdue to paintings

- Being unnecessarily argumentative

- Gossiping

- Failure to do administrative responsibilities

- Sickness absence

Your first experience of control is possibly to be inside the scope of obligation of your supervisor or his supervisor's scope. Remember that there may be some fact that managers have a tendency to sell human beings like themselves. This doesn't suggest that you want to behave like a identical to your manager but you do at least need to have a fantastic relationship and percentage a few not unusual floor.